Monica Speaks

Also by Joey Green

Monica Speaks

Genuine Pearls of Wisdom
from America's Most Famous
White House Intern

Joey Green

**Andrews McMeel
Publishing**

Kansas City

www.andrewsmcmeel.com

ISBN: 0-8362-1938-4

98 99 00 01 02 BIN 10 9 8 7 6 5 4 3 2 1

Library of Congress Catalog Card Number: 98-89261

Book design by Joey Green.
Composition by Top Dog Design

This book is dedicated to
President Bill Clinton
(depending upon what the
meaning of the word "is" is).

Introduction

Have you ever found yourself in a tough situation and asked yourself, "What would Monica Lewinsky do if she were in my shoes?"

I know I have.

That's why I compiled this book—to put Monica's timeless advice, inspiring philosophy, candid life lessons, and brilliant talking points in one convenient compendium.

In interviews and depositions before the Office of the Independent Counsel, testimony before the grand jury, E-mails to friends, and telephone conversations with Linda Tripp, Monica Lewinsky courageously told it like it is. She enriched us all with her scintillating gems of wisdom, profound insights, and unique perspective on life. From the joys of "loud rad sex" to the perils of battling "meanies," Monica Lewinsky speaks to the White House Intern within us all—with refreshing candor, affection, warmth, and intensity.

This treasure trove of Lewinsky Wit (collected here for the first time and categorized for your convenience) can be a source of inspiration, helping you and your loved ones to better cope with life's unforeseen trials and tribulations. True, you may never actually find yourself performing oral sex on the President of the United States and then revealing all the details to a grand jury because a friend illegally recorded your telephone conversations and betrayed your confidence. But we all stumble. We all endure hardships. We all do things we wish we hadn't done—some improper, some inappropriate.

Savor these words of wisdom, let them roll on your tongue like a fine cigar, and you will intimately understand why Monica Lewinsky will inevitably take her rightful place alongside Walt Whitman as the voice of a generation.

—*Joey Green*

Quotations from Monica Lewinsky

Accomplishments

"Most of my tenure at the White House I was having a relationship with the President."

—Grand jury testimony,
August 20, 1998

Achievements

"I have lied my entire life."

—Telephone conversation with Linda Tripp,
between October 3 and December 22, 1997

Addiction

"I told him that I really cared about him, and he told me that he didn't want to get addicted to me and he didn't want me to get addicted to him."

—Grand jury testimony,
August 6, 1998

Adultery

"I don't think it's right, it's not right to have an affair with a married man. I never expected to fall in love with the President. I was surprised that I did."

—Grand jury testimony,
August 20, 1998

Affairs of State

"I asked Mr. Jordan if he thought the President would always be married to the First Lady and he said, 'Yes, as he should be,' and gave me a quote from the Bible. And a few—maybe a minute or so later, he said, 'Well, maybe you two will have an affair when he's out of office.' And at that point, I was shocked because I thought Mr. Jordan had known that we had already had this affair."

—Grand jury testimony,
August 6, 1998

Allegiance

"Even if I hadn't been a low level political appointee, I thought it was probably appropriate to align myself with the President's side, being that that's whose side I was on and there was no question in my mind."

—*Grand jury testimony,*
August 6, 1998

Ambition

"After we had engaged in oral sex for a while and he stopped me as he normally did, . . . I said to him, 'You know, I really—I want to make you come.'"

—*Grand jury testimony,*
August 6, 1998

American Ingenuity

"If I were you, I would say: 'Well, I don't, I might have, but I don't remember.' That's the phrase. That's the phrase my lawyer told me. Everything is, 'I might have, but I don't remember.' 'Were you ever alone with the President?' 'Um, it's possible I may have taken him a letter on the weekend, but, you know, I might have, but I don't really—'"

—Telephone conversation with Linda Tripp, between October 3 and December 22, 1997

Answering Machine Messages

"They're pretty innocuous. Sometimes—or one time, it was, you know, 'Sorry I missed you.' One time, it was just 'Hello.' And then one time he called really late at night when I was not at home and it was whispered kind of loudly, you know, 'Come on. It's me.' Something like that. It was always nice to hear his voice."

—*Grand jury testimony,*
August 6, 1998

Architecture

"I've already had the experience of working in a yucky building."

—*E-mail to a friend,*
November 5, 1997

Art Appreciation

"I just *love* the hat pin. It is vibrant, unique, and a beautiful piece of art. My only hope is that I have a hat fit to adorn it (ahhh, I see another excuse to go shopping)!"

—*Letter to the President,*
March 2, 1997

Aspiration

"I'm going to the White House to get my presidential knee pads."

—*Reportedly to Kathlyn Bleiler*
before leaving Portland, Oregon,
to move to Washington, D.C., 1995

Attributes

"I will never do anything to hurt you. I am simply not that kind of person."

—Letter to the President,
October 1997

Authenticity

"I also—I think I wore the dress out to dinner that night, so which is why I'm not sure that that's what it is. . . . So it could be spinach dip or something. I don't know."

—Grand jury testimony,
August 6, 1998

Bad Hair Days

"Boy, I look so scary today. People might think that I thought it was Halloween."

—E-mail to Linda Tripp,
March 5, 1997

Beliefs

"I believe I used a tissue sometimes to wipe off my lipstick."

—Grand jury testimony,
August 6, 1998

"I believe that he touched me first with my underwear on, and then placed his hand under my underwear. And I think at some point, I, I removed them."

—Deposition,
August 26, 1998

Berets

"I was having a bad hair day, and this was actually the first time that I had the infamous beret on. And so I just said something to him about feeling stupid. Here I was standing here in this dumb hat, and he said that it wasn't a dumb hat, that I looked cute and he liked it."

—Deposition,
August 26, 1998

The Bible

"I read Psalm 21 about a million times."

—Grand jury testimony,
August 20, 1998

Bliss

"Things have been crazy with the creep, though I did have a wonderful visit with him on Saturday. When he doesn't put his walls up, it is always so heavenly."

—E-mail to a friend,
December 9, 1997

Bridge to the Twenty-First Century

"Nobody knows what will happen in the future."

—Letter to the President,
October 1997

Briefings

"Sometimes I would put together jokes I got on the Internet or e-mail jokes that I put together for him because, you know, everyone needs to laugh, so—I think maybe—maybe there was a time that I said, 'Oh, you should look at these jokes, they're really funny.'"

—Grand jury testimony,
August 20, 1998

British History

"Bill, I loved you with all my heart. I wanted to be with you all of the time. Most recently in London, I walked the streets thinking how content I would be to walk the streets at your side while you spoke of things past—filled the air and my soul with your knowledge of history."

—Letter to the President,
October 1997

Burden of Proof

"Well, part of the problem is that instead of just saying 'I don't like you anymore,' he pulled all this other [stuff]. So it's now become, you know, my obsession to prove him wrong, you know. . . . 'Cause, really, he's not trying to be good, and he just doesn't like me. . . . So he should just say that. And—because, of course, I don't know, somehow that'll make me feel better."

—Telephone conversation with
Linda Tripp, between October 3
and December 22, 1997

Cabinet Appointments

"I'll never forget when he [President Clinton] said something or another to me, he said, 'Well, you can, you know, go wherever you want—well, within reason.' Well, that's what he said to me. And I—you know, I thought to myself—I didn't say it, I bit my tongue—but I was thinking, 'No, you *(redacted)*, I'm gonna say I want to be Chief of Staff.'"

—Telephone conversation with
Linda Tripp, between October 3 and
December 22, 1997

Caller I.D.

"When he called from the Oval Office, the phones have a caller I.D. up at the top, and when he calls from the Oval Office it says POTUS and when he calls from the residence it has an asterisk. . . . I think one time when he called and I picked up the phone I said something that indicated to him that I knew who it was. And he said, 'Well, how did you know it was me?' And I told him, 'Well, don't you know that it lights up POTUS when you call from the Oval Office?' And he said, 'No, I didn't know that.' So I thought that was funny."

—*Grand jury testimony,*
August 6, 1998

Camaraderie

"The main feeling I had had at that point, once I had received my subpoena [in the Paula Jones case] was that—that now she [Linda Tripp] didn't need to worry about denying that she knew anything about this relationship, because I was going to deny it under oath as well."

—Grand jury testimony,
August 6, 1998

Campaign Promises

"He told me that he thought that my being transferred had something to do with him and that he was upset. He said, 'Why do they have to take you away from me? I trust you.' And then he told me—he looked at me and he said, 'I promise you if I win in November I'll bring you back like that.'"

—Grand jury testimony,
August 6, 1998

Certainty

"I'm 99.9 percent certain."

—Deposition,
August 26, 1998

Character

"I could not live with myself if I caused trouble.... That is not my nature. I am a good person."

—Telephone conversation with
Linda Tripp, between October 3 and
December 22, 1997

Chemistry

"We talked briefly and sort of acknowledged that there had been a chemistry that was there before and that we were both attracted to each other and then he asked me if he could kiss me."

—Grand jury testimony,
August 6, 1998

Cigars

"After we had been intimate and we were talking in the Oval Office, he was chewing on a cigar. And then he had the cigar in his hand and he was kind of looking at the cigar in a, sort of a naughty way. And so I, I looked at the cigar and I looked at him and I said, 'We can do that, too, sometime.' And I don't, I don't really remember how it got started, but."

—*Deposition,*
August 26, 1998

Civil Disobedience

"I'm never going to come forward with this . . . and if someone else did, I would deny, deny, deny."

—*Telephone conversation with*
Linda Tripp, between October 3 and
December 22, 1997

Civil Rights

"I sit here stressed out because I know that if you don't see me tonight, by the time I do see you it will have been at least two months. What kind of message does that send to me? Have you had any desire to talk to me? Do you now wonder what's going on in my life? Do you miss me at all? Had you not brought me back such a wonderfully extravagant gift, I would be mourning the loss of you in my life. Instead, I am confused."

—*Letter to the President,*
October 1997

Clarity

"If I'm saying something and I'm not clear, I'm not understanding, just let me know, because I do that a lot."

—*Grand jury testimony,*
August 6, 1998

Cleanliness

"It may sound silly, I have a lot of clothes. I don't clean all my clothes right after I wear them, I usually don't clean them until I know I'm going to wear them again."

—Grand jury testimony,
August 20, 1998

Closeness

"He touched my breasts through clothing, being my bra, and then also without my bra on."

—Deposition,
August 26, 1998

Cocktail Reception

"He [the President] had this big 50th birthday party at Radio City Music Hall and there was a cocktail reception and at the—when he came to do the rope line and he—after he greeted me and talked to me, he was talking to a whole bunch of people in and around my area and I had . . . my back to him and I just kind of put—put my hand behind me and touched him [in the crotch area]."

—*Grand jury testimony,*
August 20, 1998

Coincidence

"I know that if the President was in the hall and he was talking to people and I passed by, he'd—he'd stop talking and say hi to me."

—Grand jury jestimony,
August 20, 1998

Collector's Items

"I had a copy of the President's book, 'Hope and History,' which he had signed to me which had a very innocuous sort of inscription."

—Grand jury testimony,
August 6, 1998

Commitment

"We had already had phone sex for the first time the week prior, and I was feeling a little bit insecure about whether he had liked it or didn't like it, and I just—I felt in general that I didn't know—from having spoken to him on the phone, you know, prior to having phone sex and from having these encounters with him, I didn't know if this was sort of developing into some kind of a longer term relationship than what I thought it initially might have been, that maybe he had some regular girlfriend who was furloughed or something during the furlough."

—*Deposition,*
August 26, 1998

Communication

"And I kind of believe in clear communication."

—*Grand jury testimony,*
August 20, 1998

Compassion

"I could certainly understand the frustrations of being told someone is going to help you get a job and then you don't."

—*Grand jury testimony,*
August 6, 1998

Compatibility

"We were very compatible sexually. And I've always felt that he was sort of my sexual soulmate, and that I just felt very connected to him when it came to those kind of things."

—*Deposition,*
August 26, 1998

Competence

"I am not a moron."

—*Letter to the President,*
November 12, 1997

Conscientious Objectors

"I didn't want to cooperate. I mean, didn't—
I just kept thinking to myself, well—well,
I'll just say I made it all up, ... I couldn't
imagine doing this to the President. And I
felt so wrong and guilty for having told
Linda [Tripp] and that she had done all this."

—*Grand jury testimony,*
August 20, 1998

Conspicuous Consumption

"I must admit it—I am a compulsive shopper!"

—Letter to the President,
March 2, 1997

Constraint

"I wasn't comfortable talking to Vernon Jordan about phone sex."

—Grand jury testimony,
August 6, 1998

Conviction

"I don't care about pretty; I care about thin. That's all I care about."

—Telephone conversation with
Linda Tripp, between October 3 and
December 22, 1997

Courage

"I was thinking today, you know, would I have the nerve—would I have the nerve to sort of whisper into the phone, you know, something like, 'I can't talk, I have someone here."

—*Telephone conversation with Linda Tripp, between October 3 and December 22, 1997*

Credentials

"I worked in a men's necktie store when I was in college for four years and so that was my thing, that was part—you know, my spending money, a lot of it came from working. And so I love ties. And I—I mean, I can pick out—you know, different designers and stuff."

—*Grand jury testimony, August 20, 1998*

Current Affairs

"We enjoyed talking to each other and being with each other. We were very affectionate. . . . We would tell jokes. We would talk about our childhoods. Talk about current events. I was always giving him my stupid ideas about what I thought should be done in the administration or different views on things. I think back on it and he always made me smile when I was with him. It was a lot of— he was sunshine."

—*Grand jury testimony,*
August 6, 1998

Dairy Products

"Did I tell you I had sex with Thomas last week? I know. I am sooooooo naughty. It was fun and good. I went over there with some ice cream and pretty much seduced him in a way that made him make the moves on me . . . cool or what???"

—*E-mail to a friend,*
August 14, 1997

Damage Control

"I thought that first Mrs. Clinton should do something publicly, maybe on a TV show or something, and talk about how difficult the [Paula Jones] case had been for her and on her daughter and that she just wished that he would settle it and it would go away. And then the President should unannounced and unexpectedly go into the briefing room, make a brief statement that he—in an effort to put this behind him, you know, against his attorneys' advice, he was going to pay Ms. Jones whatever it was, however much she wanted, and so that this case would be over with."

—Grand jury testimony,
August 6, 1998

Danger

"I would not cross these, these people for fear of my life, number one."

—Telephone conversation with Linda Tripp, between October 3 and December 22, 1997

Decency

"I had wanted him to say that I was a nice, decent person and that he was sorry this had happened because I—I tried to do as much as I could to protect him. I mean, I didn't— I didn't—I didn't allow him to be put on tape that night."

—Grand jury testimony, August 20, 1998

Decorum

"I wouldn't ever wear red lipstick to see him."

—Telephone conversation with Linda Tripp, between October 3 and December 22, 1997

Deductive Reasoning

"Handsome, you have been distant the past few months and have shut me out; I don't know why. Is it that you don't like me anymore or are you scared?"

> —*Undated draft of a letter to the President recovered from a deleted computer file, 1997*

Defamation

"Linda Tripp called me at work on October 6th and told me that her friend Kate in the NSC [National Security Council] had heard from—had heard rumors about me and that I would never work in the White House again and, if I did, I wouldn't have a blue pass and that her advice to me was 'Get out of town.' So that meant to me that I wasn't going to be coming back to the White House and I was very upset by that."

> —*Grand jury testimony, August 6, 1998*

Deficit Spending

"A month before she [Linda Tripp] had had no money for the bus and was trying to sell her clothes and somehow she had $500 to spend on food [for a Christmas party] and had money to spend on presents underneath her tree and it was just dumb."

—*Grand jury testimony,*
August 6, 1998

Democracy

"He has a problem and we, the American people, elected him, so let him do his stupid job. You know?"

—*Telephone conversation with*
Linda Tripp, between October 3 and
December 22, 1997

Demographics

"I've always categorized people as people who are there to serve the President and people who are there to serve themselves through the President."

—*Grand jury testimony,*
August 6, 1998

Detachment

"It was awful when I saw you for your birthday in August. You were so distant that I missed you as I was holding you in my arms."

—*Letter to the President,*
November 12, 1997

Devotion

"I feel very connected to you and I have no idea why. I have often told you in person and on paper the various things you mean to me and my feelings for you. I have detailed the ways in which I think you are an incredible man—despite what you may have done in the past or do now that hurt people you care about. I know you and what you have been through."

—Letter to the President,
October 1997

Dignity

"We were never physically intimate in the Oval Office."

—Grand jury testimony,
August 6, 1998

Diplomacy

"I didn't really want the job [with Ambassador Bill Richardson at the United Nations]. And so I sort of just 'yessed' him along and thanked him profusely, and told him I was excited about it."

—Deposition,
August 26, 1998

Directness

"I asked him why he doesn't ask me any questions about myself, and doesn't he, you know, is this just about sex, you know, because if it is, then I just want to know that; or do you have some interest in trying to get to know me as a person."

—Deposition,
August 26, 1998

Disappointment

"You let me down, but I shouldn't have trusted you in the first place."

—Unsent letter to the President,
September 1997

Disaster Relief

"I am depressed. I float from being sad to angry often and easily. What can I do but weather the storm?"

—E-mail to a friend,
May 18, 1997

Discrimination

"I don't think people necessarily talk about these things. I mean, there is a difference between a relationship that you have with someone who is sort of involved in a situation, and then the kind of relationship you have with a friend whom you talk to."

—Grand jury testimony,
August 6, 1998

Dissent

"It wasn't as if the President called me and said, 'You know, Monica, you're on the witness list, this is going to be really hard for us, we're going to have to tell the truth and be humiliated in front of the entire world about what we've done,' which I would have fought him on probably."

—Grand jury testimony,
August 6, 1998

Dissociation

"I have always been one of those people who has never wanted to be the one to end a relationship because I learned at an early age that I regret."

—Letter to the President,
October 1997

Divestment

"We were in the back office and we were kissing, and I was—I had a dress on that buttoned all the way, all the way up and down. . . . It was long and down to the, to my ankles, or whatever. And he unbuttoned my dress and he unhooked my bra, and sort of took the dress off of my shoulders and took the bra off of my, off of my—I'm not explaining this right. So that he moved the bra so that my bra was kind of hanging on one shoulder and so was off. And he just was, he was looking at me and touching me and telling me how beautiful I was."

—Deposition,
August 26, 1998

Double Entendres

"I was just concerned that they [White House staff members] would purposefully say something different from whatever I said just because they had the opportunity to screw me. I mean—not—never mind. To cause trouble for me. How's that?"

—Grand jury testimony,
August 6, 1998

Double Standards

"I've always felt that some of the, some of the staffers there, particularly [Deputy Chief of Staff] Evelyn Lieberman and those who worked with her to move me out of the White House, instead—looked at my behavior only, instead of looking at the President's behavior, and instead of necessarily thinking that I had a relationship with the President, were just looking at it thinking I was trying to have a relationship with the President when I was already having a relationship with him. They turned a blind eye to his actions."

*—Deposition,
August 26, 1998*

Dreams

"Nothing would make me happier than to see you, except to see you naked with a winning lottery ticket in one hand and a can of whipped cream in the other."

—Text of a postcard to the President,
December 7, 1997

Dress Codes

"I don't know if I ever told Linda [Tripp] I gave my mom the blue dress. One of the things I did say was that I gave everything to my mom, so that probably included that and that was not true. I didn't give the evidence to my mom. My mom never hid the dress. She didn't know it was in New York."

—Grand jury testimony,
August 20, 1998

Dress for Success

"Oh, he went to go put his hand down my pants, and then I unzipped them because it was easier. And I didn't have any panties on. And so he manually stimulated me."

—Deposition,
August 26, 1998

Due Process

"I didn't understand why they—why they had to trap me into coming there, why they had to trick me into coming there. I mean, this had all been a set-up and that's why—I mean, that was just so frightening. It was so incredibly frightening. And they told me, you know, over and over again I was free to leave whenever I wanted, but—I—I didn't—I didn't know that there's a grand jury and [*sic*] indicted and then you go to jail. I mean, and a trial and everything. I didn't understand that."

—Grand jury testimony,
August 20, 1998

Education

"He was just very sweet, and he—when I got up to leave, he kissed my arm and told me he'd call me, and then I said, 'Yeah, well, what's my phone number?' And so he recited both my home number and my office number off the top of his head. So, I told him, you know, that he got an A."

—*Deposition,*
August 26, 1998

Efficiency

"I've always been a date-oriented person and I had a—probably a habit of circling dates in my Filofax when I either talked to the President or saw him."

—*Grand jury testimony,*
August 6, 1998

Election Results

"I was so sure that the weekend after the election you would call me to come visit and you would kiss me passionately and tell me you couldn't wait to have me back."

—Unsent letter to the President,
September 1997

Encouragement

"For me, the best way to explain how I feel what happened was, you know, no one asked or encouraged me to lie, but no one discouraged me either."

—Grand jury testimony,
August 6, 1998

Energy

"I want to be a source of pleasure and laughter and energy to you. I want to make you smile."

—Letter to the President,
October 1997

Epiphany

"Oh, my God, Linda, he looked so *(redacted)* gorgeous."

—Telephone conversation with Linda Tripp,
between October 3 and December 22, 1997,
describing the President

Equal Rights

"We would joke with each other sexually. And so sometimes, you know, I might hit him on the butt, or he might hit me on the butt."

—*Deposition,*
August 26, 1998

E.S.P.

"I don't know if it was ever verbally spoken but it was understood between the President and myself that . . . most people weren't in on the weekends so . . . it would be safer to do that then."

—*Grand jury testimony,*
August 6, 1998

Etiquette

"I think we were both aware of the volume and sometimes I'd use my hand—I bit my hand—so that I wouldn't make any noise."

—Grand jury testimony,
August 6, 1998

Evidence

"And she [Linda Tripp] told me that I should put it [the dress] in a safe deposit box because it could be evidence one day. And I said that was ludicrous because I would never—I would never disclose that I had a relationship with the President, I would never need it."

—Grand jury testimony,
August 20, 1998

Executive Privilege

"We were kissing and he lifted my sweater and exposed my breasts and was fondling them with his hands and with his mouth. And then I believe I was fondling him over his pants in his genital area, and I think again I tried to unbutton his pants and I couldn't. So, he did it."

—Deposition,
August 26, 1998

Exile

"The worst thing you could do to me is cease all contact and banish me from your life."

—Letter to the President,
October 1997

Existentialism

"I feel disposable, used, and insignificant."

—Letter to the President,
June 29, 1997

Failure

"It just is an upsetting, uncomfortable, unsettling feeling when your backup has turned into your only option."

—Telephone conversation with
Linda Tripp, between October 3 and
December 22, 1997

Family Values

"Well, my mom knew, you know, that I was having some sort of a relationship with the President. My dad had no idea."

—Grand jury testimony,
August 6, 1998

Famine

"There were topics that I wanted to stay away from and the time that I spent with him was precious to me. So things that were unpleasant I didn't bring up unless I had to."

—*Grand jury testimony,*
August 20, 1998

Famous Last Words

"I would just like to say that no one ever asked me to lie and I was never promised a job for my silence. And that I'm sorry. I'm really sorry for everything that's happened. And I hate Linda Tripp."

—*Grand jury testimony,*
August 20, 1998

Fantasy

"That's what I want. You know, that's my fantasy, is to have him wear one of my ties every day."

—Telephone conversation with Linda Tripp, between October 3 and December 22, 1997

Fatigue

"I got upset and I decided that I was really tired of everything that was going on and I just—it was clear to me that he was ignoring me and I just didn't want to deal with this anymore."

—Grand jury testimony, August 6, 1998

Faux Pas

"I think there had been at least one time when Betty [Currie]'s pager had been sitting on her desk when she was in with the President or had stepped away and someone else had picked up her pager when it went off and there was a message from me. And so from—you know, Betty kind of covered it, I think by saying—or she did actually have another friend named Monica or something or another."

—Grand jury testimony,
August 6, 1998

Fidelity

"I don't believe for one minute that he is being good. . . . I really don't. I thought—I said to myself, I said, 'Okay I will believe he's being good if he calls me, and we have phone sex, okay, like while this stress is going on' . . . because then I know he's trying to be as good as he can be."

—Telephone conversation with Linda Tripp,
between October 3 and December 22, 1997

Finger on the Button

"I believe he took a phone call in his office, so we moved from the hallway into the back office, and the lights were off. And at that point, he, he put his hand down my pants and stimulated me manually in the genital area."

—Deposition, August 26, 1998

Foreign Intervention

"I was in the middle of saying something and he just started kissing me. And, so, it was funny. It was, it was very funny."

—Deposition, August 26, 1998

Foreign Policy

"I asked him if we could, if we could share a birthday kiss in honor of our birthdays, because mine had been just a few weeks before. So, he said that that was okay and we could kind of bend the rules that day. And so we, we, we kissed. And then I was touching him in his genital area through his shorts, and then I, I went to [perform oral sex] . . . and he wouldn't let me. . . . He got upset when I, you know, when he stopped me and he said, 'I'm trying to not do this and I'm trying to be good.' And he, he got visibly upset. And so I, I hugged him and I told him I was sorry and not to be upset, and I was a little shocked, actually. I didn't—he seemed to get so emotionally upset about it. It seemed a little bit strange to me."

—*Deposition,*
August 26, 1998

Formality

LEWINSKY: Can you guys call me Monica? Are they allowed to call me Monica instead of Ms. Lewinsky? I was just—

FOREMAN: If you say so.

LEWINSKY: . . . I'm just 25. Please.

JUROR: But you'll always be Ms. Lewinsky, whether you're 25 or 28 or . . . .

LEWINSKY: Not if I get married.

—Grand jury testimony,
August 20, 1998

Freedom of Expression

"There were on some occasions when I sent him cards or notes that I wrote things that he deemed too personal to put on paper just in case something ever happened, if it got lost getting there or someone else opened it. So there were several times when he remarked to me, you know, you shouldn't put that on paper."

—Grand jury testimony,
August 6, 1998

Freedom of Information

"It was never, ever, ever my intention for this relationship to ever become public."

—Deposition,
August 26, 1998

Freeing the Captive

"We were kissing and he unbuttoned my dress and fondled my breasts with my bra on, and then took them out of my bra and was kissing them and touching them with his hands and with his mouth."

—*Deposition,*
August 26, 1998

Freud

"Linda, I almost called you mom."

—*Telephone conversation with*
Linda Tripp, between October 3 and
December 22, 1997

Friendliness

"I'm a friendly person and—and I didn't know it was a crime in Washington for people—for you to want people to like you and so I was friendly. And I guess I wasn't supposed to be."

—Grand jury testimony,
August 20, 1998

Furloughs

"When this first happened, I mean, I said to my mom, I said, 'Well, I think he just fooled around with me because his girlfriend was probably furloughed.'"

—Telephone conversation with
Linda Tripp, between October 3 and
December 22, 1997

Futility

"I asked you three weeks ago to please be sensitive to what I am going through right now and to keep in contact with me, and yet I'm still left writing notes in vain."

—*Letter to the President,*
November 12, 1997

Generation Gap

"Jeez . . . I hate being called 'dear.' The creep calls me that sometimes [*sic*] it's an old person saying!!!!"

—*E-mail to a friend,*
August 14, 1997

Generosity

"I enclosed a card [with a gift] wishing him a fun vacation and asked in a post script if he could bring me a 'Black Dog' t-shirt, which you probably know is from this quasi-famous restaurant in Martha's Vineyard—if he had a chance. Well, I found out from Betty [Currie] yesterday that he not only brought me a t-shirt, he got me 2 t-shirts, a hat and a dress!!!! Even though he's a big schmuck that is surprisingly sweet—even that he remembered!"

—E-mail to a friend,
September 16, 1997

Girl Talk

"What I said to Linda [Tripp] was, 'Oh, you know, I told—I told Mr. Jordan that I wasn't going to sign the affidavit until I got the job.' Obviously, which wasn't true. I told her I didn't yet have a job. That wasn't true. I told her I hadn't signed the affidavit. That wasn't true. I told her that some time over the holidays I had freaked out and my mom took me to Georgetown Hospital and they put me on Paxil. That wasn't true. I think I told her that—you know, at various times the President and Mr. Jordan had told me I had to lie. That wasn't true. That's just a small example. Probably some more things about my mom. Linda had an obsession with my mom, so she was a good leverage."

—*Grand jury testimony,*
August 6, 1998

Good Judgment

"He [the President] told me he was going to watch a movie with some friends of his and that if I wanted to I could bump into him in the hall outside and then he'd invite me into the movie. . . . I think he said there were some friends and maybe some of his staff or I asked him if some of his staff was going to be there. And he said yes and I don't remember who he said was going to be there, but I said I didn't think that was a good idea."

—Grand jury testimony,
August 20, 1998

Gratitude

"A little phrase (with only eight letters) like 'thank you' simply cannot begin to express what I feel for what you have given me."

—Letter to the President,
March 2, 1997

Grievances

"And Mr. Jordan asked me what I got angry at the President about, so I told him when he doesn't call me enough or see me enough."

—Grand jury testimony,
August 6, 1998

Guilt

"And not only do we not have phone sex, I don't even *(redacted)* hear from him. And I think that's his guilt. I think he feels guilty. Because he's with other people."

—*Telephone conversation with Linda Tripp, between October 3 and December 22, 1997*

Homage

"It's a really nice tie, and I—you know, at first I said, 'Oh, you know,' I said, 'it'll look good with either a taupe or navy suit and a white or—white, blue shirt, whatever you want. . . . ' And, you know, I'm like 'That is if you like it.' And I'm like, 'And just think now you can pay homage to me if you want by having a work week in which you wear one of my ties everyday.'"

—*Telephone conversation with Linda Tripp, between October 3 and December 22, 1997*

Homophobia

"When I was leaving [Vernon Jordan's office], I asked him if he would give the President a hug for me. I bugged him again about making sure he told the President. And so he said, 'I don't hug men.' I said, 'Well, okay.'"

—*Grand jury testimony,*
August 6, 1998

Honorable Intentions

"I asked him why he doesn't ask me any questions about myself, and doesn't he, you know, is this just about sex, you know, because if it is, then I just want to know that; or do you have some interest in trying to get to know me as a person."

—*Deposition,*
August 26, 1998

Hostility

"I don't know if anyone here has ever done this, where you—you're annoyed with someone so you kind of want to pick a fight with them and you want to be a little bit hostile so that—you know, you just rub them the wrong way."

—Grand jury testimony,
August 6, 1998

The Hotline

"He was on the telephone while he was . . . touching me, and was also on the telephone when I was performing oral sex."

—Deposition, August 26, 1998

Human Nature

"Because if you *(redacted)* people over, they're going to turn around and *(redacted)* you."

—Telephone conversation with Linda Tripp, between October 3 and December 22, 1997

Hypocrisy

"And then I said, . . . 'Well, don't you get any warmth and da da da from your wife?' . . . He said, 'Of course I do.'"

—Telephone conversation with Linda Tripp, between October 3 and December 22, 1997

Impetus

"Oh, my gosh. This is so embarrassing. . . .
Can I hide under the table? Uh—I had—I
had wanted—I tried to—I placed his genital
next to mine and had hoped that if he—
oh—this is just too embarrassing. . . . Then I,
not that we would have intercourse that day,
but that that might make him want to."

—*Grand jury testimony,*
August 20, 1998

Inalienable Rights

"The President wasn't responding to me and wasn't returning my calls and wasn't responding to my notes. And I got very upset so I sat down that morning actually and scribbled out a long letter to him that talked about my frustrations and that he had promised to bring me back; if he wasn't going to bring me back that I—you know, then could he help me find a job."

—Grand jury testimony,
August 6, 1998

Inaugurations

"Sometimes he initiated it, sometimes I initiated it. . . . It didn't necessarily go though my mind, okay, now it's time to perform oral sex."

—Deposition,
August 26, 1998

Indecision

"To top it all off the big creep is wearing one of my ties today. I think I'm just going to have to walk away from it all. I don't know yet. I know it's annoying—I'm always saying this and then I change my mind."

—*E-mail to a friend,*
May 18, 1997

Indebtedness

"Because he had sort of led me to believe that he was going to bring me back and was constantly reassuring that, I, I believe that he did owe that to me. Versus him having said, I'm really sorry . . . that this happened, there's not, you know, there's nothing I can do, and left it at that. Then I wouldn't have felt that he owed me anything."

—*Deposition,*
August 26, 1998

Independence Day

"At one point, we, we had been talking about—I made some remarks to him about his relationship with Mrs. Clinton. And he, he remarked a little bit later than that that he wished he had more time for me. And so I said, 'Well, maybe you will have more time in three years.' And I was actually sort of thinking just when he wasn't President, he was going to have more time on his hands. And he said, 'Well, I don't know, I might be alone in three years.'"

—Deposition,
August 26, 1998

Individuality

"I did see the cutest boy in the elevator yesterday. At Bloomingdale's. He was so cute. . . . I like, you know, I like guys who have—he had a big scar on his forehead. And I like that. I do. I just, I like somebody who looks a little different. You know what I mean?"

—*Telephone conversation with Linda Tripp,*
between October 3 and December 22, 1997

Ingenuity

"I made an effort on my own to go out a different door than the door that I came in so that if there was a guard that was on duty in the front of the Oval Office he might see me going in but a different guard would see me leave, so no one would know exactly how long I had been in there."

—*Grand jury testimony,*
August 6, 1998

Initiative

"The President and I were in—I believe it was the back study or the study and—or we might have been in the hallway, I don't really remember, but I—[Presidential Advisor] Harold Ickes has a very distinct voice and so he—I heard him holler 'Mr. President,' and the President looked at me and I looked at him and he jetted out into the Oval Office and I panicked and didn't know that—I thought that maybe because Harold was so close with the President that they might just wander back there and the President would assume that I knew to leave. So I went out the back way."

—Grand jury testimony,
August 6, 1998

Inner Peace

"I just wish I didn't have all this emotional stuff. I wish I could be like him. . . . I guarantee you he has not gone through one ounce of pain having to do with me in the past six, seven months. He just threw it all away, you know?"

—Telephone conversation with
Linda Tripp, between October 3 and
December 22, 1997

Inquisitiveness

"I'm just nosy."

—Telephone conversation with
Linda Tripp, between October 3 and
December 22, 1997

Insecurity

"I'm an insecure person and ... I was insecure about the relationship at times and thought that he would come to forget me easily and if I hadn't heard from him—especially after I left the White House, it was—it was very difficult for me ... and usually when I'd see him, it would kind of prompt him to call me. So I made an effort. I would go early [to public functions] and stand in the front so I could see him, blah, blah, blah."

—Grand jury testimony,
August 20, 1998

Insight

"I was really nervous because I hadn't been alone with the President since the elections so I was...kind of internal, focused on being nervous."

—Grand jury testimony,
August 6, 1998

Integrity

"I had left the White House like a good girl in April of '96. A lot of other people might have made a really big stink and said that they weren't going to lose their job and they didn't want to do that and would have talked about what kind of relationship they had with the President so they didn't lose their job."

—Grand jury testimony,
August 6, 1998

Intellectual Pursuits

"Ohhh how I long for the time when we can just spend a day together...starting w/ coffee at Starbucks...shopping...lunch at somewhere yummy...maybe a movie... more shopping...and then getting drunk on margaritas!!! Whooo-hoooo!"

—E-mail to a friend,
November 6, 1997

Intentions

"My intention had really been to come to Washington and start over, and I didn't want to have another affair with a married man because it was really painful. It was horrible. And I feel even worse about it now."

—Grand jury testimony,
August 20, 1998

Interaction

"Oh, we spent hours on the phone talking. It was emotional. . . . I mean, we were talking. I mean, interaction. I mean, talking about what we were thinking and feeling and doing and laughing."

—*Grand jury testimony, August 20, 1998*

Internal Affairs

"He spent a lot of time talking to me. He was very, very—he was the most affectionate with me he'd ever been. There wasn't a second when he wouldn't be touching me, whether it was holding my hand or stroking my arm or, you know, he'd kiss my neck at one point. It was just—or he'd, you know, put his hands, he was running his hands through my hair and touching my face. And my bra strap kept falling down my shoulder. So, he kept pushing my bra strap up. It was just very—it was intense. It was just really emotionally intense."

—*Deposition, August 26, 1998*

International Affairs

"The Richardson thing [job at the United Nations] does sound interesting for someone who likes international affairs—NOT ME."

> —*E-mail to a friend,*
> *November 6, 1997*

Intimidation

"I just thought, you know, 'I don't deal with you like the President, I deal with you as a person.'"

> —*Grand jury testimony,*
> *August 6, 1998*

Isolation

"This is so hard for me. I am trying to deal with so much emotionally, and I have nobody to talk to about it."

—Letter to the President,
November 12, 1997

Issues

"Ties were a big issue with us and I used to bug him all the time on the phone, 'Well, when are you going to wear one of my ties?' You know. Or he'd say, 'Did you see—' On one occasion, I remember specifically he said, 'Did you see I wore your tie the other day?' . . . And I used to say to him that 'I like it when you wear my ties because then I know I'm close to your heart.'"

—Grand jury testimony,
August 20, 1998

Jealousy

"I had—from some of my conversations with Linda [Tripp], I started to think that she was a little bit jealous that Mr. Jordan was helping me get a job in New York and that I was leaving the Pentagon and that—she had remarked one time that—that, you know, Mr. Jordan who is the most powerful, you know, man in this city got me my attorney and she—she thinks that she only had—you know, this dinky attorney or something like that."

—Grand jury testimony,
August 6, 1998

Job Descriptions

"He [Legislative Affairs Deputy Tim Keating] told me I was too sexy to be working in the East Wing and that this job at the Pentagon where I'd be writing press releases was a sexier job."

—Grand jury testimony,
August 6, 1998

Job Interviews

"I think everyone can relate to having a bad interview. Maybe."

—Grand jury testimony,
August 6, 1998

Job Rating

"Well, he's done a damn good job of controlling himself around me."

—Telephone conversation with
Linda Tripp, between October 3 and
December 22, 1997

Job Security

"And she [Linda Tripp] said, 'Monica, promise me you won't sign the affidavit until you get the job. Tell Vernon [Jordan] you won't sign the affidavit until you get the job because if you sign the affidavit before you get the job, they're never going to give you the job.'"

—Grand jury testimony,
August 6, 1998

Kathleen Willey

"She could have, you know, smeared her own lipstick and untucked her own blouse."

—Grand jury testimony,
August 6, 1998

Keepsakes

"I put all the gifts that he had given me on my bed and I got a big box from The Gap and went through each item and decided if I needed to give it to them or not. . . . It sort of was a difficult—I—I wasn't sure if I was going to get this box back, so I didn't want to give everything in the event that I didn't get the box back for some reason. And I kept out some innocuous things and I kept out the—really the most—the most sentimental gift he had given me was the book, the 'Leaves of Grass' book, so—and it was just—it's beautiful and it meant a lot to me, so I kept that one."

—Grand jury testimony,
August 6, 1998

Leadership

"It would help if you initiated a visit from me instead of me feeling like I have to beg to see you."

—Undated draft of a letter to the President
recovered from a deleted computer file, 1997

Legal Opinions

"I thought Paula Jones' claim was bunk and I didn't want to be associated with the case."

—Grand jury testimony,
August 6, 1998

Legalities

"I thought that signing an affidavit could range from anywhere—the point of it would be to deter or to prevent me from being deposed and so that that could range from anywhere between maybe just somehow mentioning, you know, innocuous things or going as far as maybe having to deny any kind of relationship."

—Grand jury testimony,
August 6, 1998

Legislative Body

PRESIDENT: I like big mugs.

LEWINSKY: No, you like big jugs.

> —*After giving a Starbucks coffee mug*
> *to the President on December 6, 1997*
> *(OIC interview, July 30, 1998)*

Levity

"There was always a lot of joking that went on between us. And so we, you know, I mean it was fun. When we were together, it was fun."

> —*Deposition,*
> *August 26, 1998*

Liberty

"We were intimate in the hallway, and then it was a phone call that prompted us to go into the office. And that when we were in the office, that, that he, he removed, he sort of removed his pants."

—*Deposition,*
August 26, 1998

Lies

"I have never—I don't—I certainly believe I have ever told a lie to hurt anybody, that I sort of—some of the ways in which I grew up, it was—there were secrets and inherent in a secret is a lie and so . . . I just thought I'd tell you that."

—*Grand jury testimony,*
August 20, 1998

Literature

"Before the creep left for his vacation I gave him a copy of the novel 'The Notebook'—it's this mushy romance (written by a guy) that is like 'Bridges of Madison County' sort of BUT one of the recurring themes or things of significance that comes up in the book is Whitman's (gee not Thoreau's—duh) 'Leaves of Grass.' I thought it was neat and sweet."

—E-mail to a friend,
September 16, 1997

Logic

"The people who work for him have trashed me, they claim they haven't said anything about me, they have smeared me and they called me stupid, they said I couldn't write, they said I was a stalker, they said I wore inappropriate clothes, I mean, you all know. I mean, you've heard them in here, you've read the papers, you've seen on TV, and yet—and then when it came out about the talking points, then somehow no one ever asked the question, well, how could—if she was so stupid and she couldn't write, how is it possible that she wrote the talking points? So then it was, well, someone must have helped her with that. Oh, it's okay, though, it wasn't someone in the White House."

—*Grand jury testimony,*
August 20, 1998

Love

"It's time for me to get out of here. I really hope that the creep and I can still have contact, because I know it sounds soooooooooo ridiculous, but I can't get him out of my heart. I love him a lot. I know it's stupid. I want to hug him so bad right now I could cry."

—E-mail to a friend,
November 6, 1997

"It started with a physical attraction, which led to a sexual relationship, and then the emotional and friendship aspects of that relationship developed after the beginning of our sexual relationship."

—Deposition,
August 26, 1998

Loyalty

"I don't know that I necessarily saw it then, but I feel now a little bit that me turning over some of these things [gifts to the President] was a little bit of an assurance to the President or reassurance that, you know, that everything was okay."

—Grand jury testimony,
August 6, 1998

Magnetism

"I'm a married man magnet."

—Telephone conversation with
Linda Tripp, between October 3 and
December 22, 1997

Man's Best Friend

"Betty [Currie] and the President and I were in the Oval Office and this was the first time I got to meet Buddy. So we played with Buddy in the office and he was running around the carpet. And I had bought a small Christmas present for Buddy. And so the three of us were just talking and goofing off."

—Grand jury testimony,
August 6, 1998

Marriage

"It sounds like such a wonderful fantasy to me. To be with your husband—as part of a couple with other couples doing couple-y kinds of things and having fun."

—E-mail to a friend,
November 5, 1997

Martyrdom

"I never told you this because I didn't want
to seem like a martyr but in April of '96 I
wanted nothing more than to beg you to do
something so I didn't have to leave. I wanted
to scream and bawl. You have no idea how
desperate, upset, humiliated I was. But I
didn't. You said you would see what you
could do and I left it at that because I didn't
want to put you in a bad situation."

—*Unsent letter to the President,*
September 1997

Means and Ways

"He unzipped his pants and sort of exposed
himself and . . . then I performed oral sex."

—*Deposition,*
August 26, 1998

Memories

"You know what's sad is it's just I'm leaving, and there is nothing I gained from this experience. He—his behavior in the past few months has really, really just eroded any, any notion I ever had of, like a pleasant memory, you know."

—Telephone conversation with
Linda Tripp, between October 3 and
December 22, 1997

Memory Loss

"I was upset, when I worked there about him. . . . I was constantly, constantly thinking he forgot who I was. . . . I was crazy. . . . I mean, it seems to me that it was like if I didn't see him, then he forgot who I was. . . . And if he didn't call, he forgot who I was."

—Telephone conversation with
Linda Tripp, between October 3 and
December 22, 1997

Men

"I don't know how guys interpret things."

—Telephone conversation with
Linda Tripp, between October 3 and
December 22, 1997

Mental Health

"I don't want you to think that I am not grateful for what you are doing for me now, I'd probably be in a mental institution without it, but I am consumed with this disappointment, frustration, and anger."

—Undated draft of a letter
to the President recovered from a
deleted computer file, 1997

Merit

"I deserve just as much as everybody else 'cause I got—sure got the *(redacted)* deal."

—Telephone conversation with
Linda Tripp, between October 3 and
December 22, 1997

Meticulousness

"I'm very particular about presents and could never give them to anyone else—they were all bought with you in mind."

—Letter to the President,
October 1997

Microsoft

"Linda [Tripp] and I had been talking and she had been talking about [how] she's really good at coming up with patterns of things or—I think that was the word she used. And so she was wanting to see—you know, I think in an effort to aid her in trying to figure out what the pattern of my relationship with the President was, I made a stupid spread-sheet on Microsoft Excel that just had the—the numbered days of the month and the months and determined on what day was there a phone call or did I see him or see him at an event or something like that."

—Grand jury testimony,
August 6, 1998

Mind over Matter

"I think he [President Clinton] talked himself out of even being attracted to me. I really
do. . . . There is just like nothing there. I mean,
it's just weird, because there was something
there last month, but there was nothing
there the other night."

—Telephone conversation with
Linda Tripp, between October 3 and
December 22, 1997

Mistrust

"I was wary of her [Linda Tripp]. I actually
thought she might have a tape recorder with
her and had looked in her bag when she had
gone up to the restroom. I told her a whole
bunch of lies that day."

—Grand jury testimony,
August 6, 1998

Modesty

"He spent a lot of time talking to me, you know, about the kind of person he thought I was, and—I'm a little bit modest. So, it's sort of—it's hard for me to get into all the things he said. . . . Just that he thought I was smart and beautiful, and that—you know, but that a lot of it, it centered around my needing to learn to, to sort of squelch a bit of the fire in my belly."

—Deposition,
August 26, 1998

Morality

"I continued to perform oral sex and then he pushed me away, kind of as he always did before he came, and then I stood up and I said, 'You know, I really, I care about you so much; I really, I don't understand why you won't let me, you know, make you come; it's important to me; I mean, it just doesn't feel complete, it doesn't seem right.'"

—Deposition,
August 26, 1998

Mother Nature

"We had discussed it and there were times when it almost happened, but mother nature was in the way."

—Grand jury testimony,
August 6, 1998,
on whether the President
performed oral sex on her

Mudslinging

"I'm only 24 and so I felt that I—this has been hard for me and this has been hard on my family and I just wanted him to take back—by saying something nice, he would have taken back every disgusting, horrible thing that anyone has said about me from that White House. And that was what I wanted."

—Grand jury testimony,
August 20, 1998

Murphy's Law

"I might get to see the Big Creep today. . . .
Of course, I have my period!!! (and am *really*
horny . . . but what else is new?)"

—Letter to a friend,
May 18, 1997

Music

"When I was hiding out in your office for a
half-hour, I noticed you had the new Sara
McLaughlin (sp?) [*sic*] CD. I have it too, and
it's wonderful. Whenever I listen to song #5
I think of you. That song and Billie Holiday's
version of 'I'll be Seeing You' are guaranteed
to put me to tears when it comes to you!"

—Undated draft of a letter
to the President recovered from a
deleted computer file, 1997

Networking

"As he was going by on the rope line shaking hands, we made eye contact and it was more intense eye contact than I had experienced before with him. . . . I mean, he—he's a charismatic person and so—just when he shook my hand and—there was an intense connection."

—Grand jury testimony,
August 6, 1998, regarding her first
encounter with the President

The New Deal

"Oh, and Handsome, remember FDR would never have turned down a visit with Lucy Mercer!"

—Letter to the President,
September 30, 1997

No-Fly Zones

"She [Deputy Chief of Staff Evelyn Lieberman] stopped me in the hall and she asked me where I worked, in which office I worked, and I told her Legislative Affairs in the East Wing. And she said, 'You're always trafficking up this area.' You know, 'You're not supposed to be here. Interns aren't allowed to go past the Oval Office.' And she—she really startled me and I walked away and I went down to the bathroom and I was crying because—I mean, when—you know, when an older woman sort of chastises you like that, it's upsetting. And then I thought about what she said and I realized that, well, I wasn't an intern anymore. I was working there."

—*Grand jury testimony,*
August 20, 1998

Nutrition

"I had a good time at the spa (I did it with the nutrition guy)!!!! Yeah! Now I can start the count over again."

—*E-mail to a friend,*
June 17, 1997

Objectives

"I just loved you—wanted to spend time with you, kiss you, listen to you laugh—and I wanted you to love me back."

—*Unsent letter to the President,*
September 1997

Obstruction of Justice

"Someone had come in at some point and he stepped out of the office, and I had put my bra and my sweater back on. And he came in and sort of made a remark about me having done that. And ... I think he smirked and he sort of said, you know, 'Damn, you put your top back on,' or something like that."

—Deposition,
August 26, 1998

Office Skills

"I believe I went to go unbutton his pants and I had trouble. So, he did that."

—Deposition,
August 26, 1998

Organization

"I'm not a very organized person. I don't clean my clothes until I'm going to wear them again."

—Grand jury testimony,
August 6, 1998

Pacifism

"All you ever have to do to pacify me is see me and hold me. Maybe that's asking too much."

—Undated draft of a
letter to the President recovered from a
deleted computer file, 1997

Pain

"I had been hurt when he referred to me as 'that woman' in January, but I was also glad. I was glad that he made that statement and I felt that was the best thing for him to do, was to deny this. And—but I had been hurt. I mean, it showed me how angry he was with me and I understood that."

—Grand jury testimony,
August 20, 1998

Paperwork Reduction Act

"I knew it would hurt to have to say goodbye to you; I just never thought it would be on paper."

—Letter to the President,
October 1997

Paranoia

"I was beyond paranoid. I mean, I—and obviously in denial. I think the—I could not understand how I had been dragged into the Paula Jones case and so I was very wary of everything."

—Grand jury testimony,
August 6, 1998

Parental Discretion

"And to my dad, what I thought about was that . . . he will be impressed with the—I think he'll be mad, too, but he'll be kind of impressed with the—just with the notion that the creep talked to his daughter—do you know what I mean?"

—Telephone conversation with
Linda Tripp, between October 3 and
December 22, 1997

Patriotism

"It's for the country. Every president, every *(redacted)* president we have ever had has always had lovers because the pressure of the job is too much. Too much. Too much to always rely on your wife, with whom you have too much baggage—which you inevitably will if you got to that point. And I think it's bad for the country."

—*Telephone conversation with Linda Tripp, between October 3 and December 22, 1997*

Peace Talks

"We were very affectionate, even when—after he broke the relationship off in May, I mean, when I'd go to visit with him, we'd—you know, we'd hug each other a lot. You know, he always used to like to stroke my hair. He—we'd hold hands. We'd smile a lot. We discussed a variety—you know, a wide range of things."

—Grand jury testimony,
August 20, 1998

Persistence

"I am so sensitive right now that I absolutely flew off the handle last week trying to get to see you (the 60 seconds was nice, but you have no idea what I had to go through just to get that; how many times I had [to] bug you-know-who)."

—Undated draft of a letter
to the President recovered from a
deleted computer file, 1997

Persuasion

"I was so desperate for her [Linda Tripp] to ... to not reveal anything about this relationship [with the President] that I used anything and anybody that I could think of as leverage with her ... Mr. Jordan, the President, my mom. Anybody that I thought would have any kind of influence on her, I used."

—*Grand jury testimony,*
August 6, 1998

Pet Peeves

"I have been peeved by the photo and the footage that was in the media from the President and First Lady being romantic on their holiday vacation. ... I was just annoyed. I was jealous and it just seemed sort of something he had never—an aspect of their relationship that he had never really revealed to me and it made me feel bad."

—*Grand jury testimony,*
August 6, 1998

Phone Sex

"He's taking care of business on one end and I'm taking care of business on another."

—*Grand jury testimony,*
August 6, 1998

Physical Therapy

"He has a bad back and so I think a lot of times we winded up just sort of standing there and talking there because he could close the door to the bathroom and lean up against the bathroom and then he was—I guess it made his back feel better and also made him a little shorter."

—*Grand jury testimony,*
August 6, 1998

Picasso

"I had a pretty boring weekend. I did, however, go with my mom to see the 'Picasso: The Early Years' exhibit yesterday. It was wonderful. I must say that I found it overwhelming to see just how much work he produced—and then to realize that was only some of his work from his EARLY years . . . jeez!!!!!"

—E-mail to a friend,
June 2, 1997

Pillow Talk

"Every time I had a visit with the President when I was working there—not after, but when I was working there—we usually would—we'd start in the back and we'd talk and that was where we were physically intimate, and we'd usually end up, kind of the pillow talk of it, I guess, was sitting in the Oval Office talking."

—Grand jury testimony,
August 6, 1998

Place in History

"And he was just angry at me and he told me ... that he had never been treated as poorly by anyone else as I treated him and that he spent more time with me than anyone else in the world, aside from his family, friends, and staff, which I don't know exactly which category that put me in."

—Grand jury testimony,
August 6, 1998

Poetry

"One time I wrote a really stupid poem."

—Grand jury testimony,
August 6, 1998

Political Connections

"When you gave me 'Leaves of Grass' I realized that the reason I was so connected to you, or so I thought, was because you were in my soul."

—*Letter to the President,*
October 1997

Politicians

"He promised me he wouldn't dump me that day. He dumped me. He promised he'd call. He didn't call. He promised to do a lot of *(redacted)* things. . . . My attitude is this: . . . I am not going to sit there and pretend he is the all mighty pristine man and he has never looked at another woman."

—*Telephone conversation with*
Linda Tripp, between October 3 and
December 22, 1997

Popularity

"There were obviously people at the White House who didn't like me and wouldn't—wouldn't be understanding of why I was coming to see the President or accepting of that."

—Grand jury testimony,
August 20, 1998

Postal System

"I mean, in general, it might have been something like me saying, well, maybe once I got there kind of saying, 'Oh, gee, here are your letters,' wink, wink, wink, and him saying, 'Okay, that's good.'"

—Grand jury testimony,
August 6, 1998

Precision

"Mr. Jordon said to me that there—'There are two important questions' or 'There are two important—' I think, 'Two important questions that are related to the [Paula Jones] case: Did you have sex with the President, you know, or did he ask?' And I said no to both of those."

—Grand jury testimony,
August 6, 1998

Predestination

"I'm the kind of person that always thinks that I can fix everything and so it was kind of this—feeling of wait, this train's going too fast and I can't stop it and that it had already passed."

—Grand jury testimony,
August 6, 1998

Predictability

"Normally, the President wouldn't call me when Mrs. Clinton was in town, so—and I usually was aware when she was out of town, so that I would sort of be expecting or hoping that he would."

—Grand jury testimony,
August 6, 1998

Preemptive Measures

"I preferred to go in through the Rose Garden because then I wasn't going—I wasn't risking the possibility of running into someone in the hall right outside the Oval Office."

—Grand jury testimony,
August 20, 1998

Preservation

"You think that I can hold onto a dress for ten, fifteen years with *(redacted)* from—"

> —Telephone conversation with Linda Tripp, between October 3 and December 22, 1997

The Presidency

"I need you right now not as President, but as a man. PLEASE be my friend."

> —Letter to the President, November 12, 1997

President Clinton

"I'm beginning to think he's just an *(redacted)* more than a moron."

> —Telephone conversation with Linda Tripp, between October 3 and December 22, 1997

Princess Diana's Death

"The Princess Di stuff. . . . I am the most sad for her sons. I think it is tragic what happened. There are a lot of people who are very upset by this whole incident. . . . I feel bad for her kids and sorry that she passed away, but I wasn't really her biggest fan—sort of neutral towards her."

—E-mail to a friend,
September 16, 1997

Principles

"Dear Schmucko, thank you for being, as my little nephew said, 'it was great to meet the principal of the United States.'"

—Telephone conversation with Linda Tripp,
between October 3 and December 22, 1997,
describing a note she sent to the President
to thank him for greeting her family

Priorities

"It was always more important to me to have him in my life than to—than to get the job, but the job was something that was important to me."

—Grand jury testimony,
August 6, 1998

Privacy

"You know, I can't answer what he [the President] was thinking, but to me, it was—there was never a question in my mind and I—from everything he said to me, I never questioned him, that we were ever going to do anything but keep this private, so that meant deny it and that meant do—take whatever appropriate steps needed to be taken."

—Grand jury testimony,
August 6, 1998

Private Sector

"I am so excited about joining the team at Revlon. I think it's going to be great!"

—Letter regarding a job offer at Revlon
that was later rescinded

Probability

"I will also be checking my messages in the hopes that the creep will call and say 'Thank you for my love note. I love you. Will you run away with me?' What do ya think the likelihood of that happening is?"

—E-mail to Linda Tripp,
February 13, 1997

Procedures

"Then once I was in my office, he called me and we made an arrangement that I would pass—he would have the door to his office open, and I would pass by the office with some papers and then he would, he would sort of stop me and invite me in. So, that was exactly what happened."

—Deposition,
August 26, 1998

Protection

"In discussions—I told him I would always —I would always deny it, I would always protect him."

—Grand jury testimony,
August 20, 1998

Protocol

"There continued to sort of be this flirtation that was—when we'd see each other."

—Grand jury testimony,
August 6, 1998

Prudence

"I tended to say things like, 'Well, when you're alone,' you know, 'Call me when you're alone,' kind of a thing or, you know, that was how we discussed sort of Mrs. Clinton maybe not being there, was, 'Well, I'll be alone on this day. Shall I—' I think we were careful—or I was careful, I know I was."

—Grand jury testimony,
August 20, 1998

Psychics

"She [Linda Tripp] told me about her—this friend, I don't remember her name, but she's this—she's an Indian woman who Linda goes to the gym with and that this Indian woman had gone to a psychic and the psychic had essentially said that one of her friends was in imminent danger having to do with the words she would speak."

—*Grand jury testimony,*
August 6, 1998

Psychology

"There's some personal and intimate aspects of a sexual relationship that develop just in talking or laughing or getting to the point where you, where you kiss someone on every encounter. But for me, I think that spending the time talking to him was certainly when I, when I got to know him as a person and started to realize that he wasn't necessarily the person I thought he was at that point."

—Deposition,
August 26, 1998

Purpose

"I asked him if we could sort of bump ... into each other in the hallway on purpose this time, because when it happened accidentally, that seemed to work really well and I felt more comfortable doing that."

—Deposition,
August 26, 1998

Pursuit of Happiness

LEWINSKY: I went back into Nancy's office to tell him the door was locked, and he was manually stimulating himself.

COUNSEL FOR THE INDEPENDENT COUNSEL: . . . And what did you do when you saw that?

LEWINSKY: I smiled.

—Deposition,
August 26, 1998

Quality Time

"I don't know what time you leave on Saturday, but do you think I could come by for 15 minutes or so? 60 seconds really didn't do it for me."

—Undated draft of a letter
to the President recovered from a
deleted computer file, 1997

Quintessence

"Art and poetry are gifts to my soul."

—*Letter to the President,*
March 2, 1997

Rainy Days

"It is an overcast, Portland-like day today and I just want to crawl into my beddy-bye and read, nap and relax. (Of course, having a boy there too wouldn't be so bad!!!)"

—*E-mail to a friend,*
November 7, 1997

Reactionaries

"There were often times when I was with Mr. Jordan that he would have no reaction at all. He would kind of do the 'Mmmph' thing."

—*Grand jury testimony,*
August 6, 1998

Real People

"Whew! What a day! I met with the big creep's best friend this morning. It was very interesting. I have never met such a 'real' person in my entire life. You know how some people where [*sic*] their hearts on their sleeves; he wears his soul. Incredible."

—*E-mail to a friend,*
November 6, 1997

Recollections

"And I don't recall how I knew that, so I don't know if maybe that's just how I'm recalling it or that I knew it and I don't remember who told me."

—*Grand jury testimony,*
August 6, 1998

Recycling

"I think that I may have had a discussion with the President about him throwing things away, I think, or making sure that they're not there. I know one specific occasion in one of the notes that I sent him I made a joke that really was reminding him not to . . . make sure he threw it away."

—Grand jury testimony,
August 6, 1998

Regret

"I just wish I could do something—I wish I could just do something that would make him go, 'Gee, I was stupid,' you know? Like, 'Boy, it was really dumb to let her go'—or something."

—Telephone conversation with
Linda Tripp, between October 3 and
December 22, 1997

Rejection

"I don't want to talk to him—I don't want to look at him. I can't look at him on TV. I can't anything."

—Telephone conversation with Linda Tripp, between October 3 and December 22, 1997

"It was so sad seeing you tonight because I was so angry with you that you once again rejected me and yet, all I wanted was for everyone else in the room to disappear and for you to hold me."

—Letter to the President, October 1997

Relativity

LEWINSKY: I saw him on like Sunday and then I said to him, I said, "Oh, look for me at the arrival ceremony on blah, blah, blah. My mom and my aunt are coming."

TRIPP: But he didn't know which was which.

LEWINSKY: No, but he, you know, he said, "I saw them. They're cute." And I said, "Shut up."

TRIPP: *(Laughs.)*

LEWINSKY: Not that cute. Like, not cuter than me.

TRIPP: I wonder what he was thinking.

LEWINSKY: How he could do them, too.

> —*Telephone conversation with Linda Tripp, between October 3 and December 22, 1997*

Remorse

"I was hurt that—that he didn't even—sort of acknowledge me in his remarks. And even also—I mean, that has to do with directly with me, but I thought he should have acknowledged all the other people that have gone through a lot of pain for seven months."

—Grand jury testimony,
August 20, 1998,
regarding President Clinton's
nationally televised apology

Repentance

"First of all I think he should have straight out apologized and I think that he could have acknowledged that—you know, apologized to me, I think, to the other people who were involved in this and to my family."

—*Grand jury testimony,*
August 20, 1998

Repulsion

"My mom would vomit if she saw him. I think she'd smack him."

—*Telephone conversation with*
Linda Tripp, between October 3 and
December 22, 1997

Respect

LEWINSKY: You know what I said at the end [of a phone call with the President]?

TRIPP: What?

LEWINSKY: . . . What's the worst thing I could say?

TRIPP: "Do you love me?"

LEWINSKY: No.

TRIPP: "I love you."

LEWINSKY: Yep.

TRIPP: You didn't.

LEWINSKY: I did. We're getting off, and I'm like, all right, "I love you, butthead." I called him butthead.

TRIPP: You didn't.

LEWINSKY: . . . I was like, oh my God, what the hell just came out of my mouth?

TRIPP: Butthead.

LEWINSKY: Butthead.

> —*Telephone conversation with Linda Tripp,*
> *between October 3 and December 22, 1997*

Responsibility

"I think no matter what—no matter how he has wronged me, no matter how many girl-friends he had, no matter how many people he abused, no matter how many, it—it was my choice."

*—Telephone conversation with Linda Tripp,
between October 3 and December 22, 1997*

"I feel very responsible for a lot of what's happened, you know, in the seven months, but I tried—I tried very hard to do what I could to not—to not hurt him."

*—Grand jury testimony,
August 20, 1998*

Restraint

"There have been many times I've wanted to defend myself and the lies that have been spewed out."

*—Grand jury testimony,
August 20, 1998*

Restricted Areas

"We were in the bathroom and I was performing oral sex. I'm sorry, this is embarrassing. And usually he doesn't want to—he didn't want to come to completion. . . . And this has sort of been a subject that we had talked about many times before and he was always saying it had issues to do with trust and not knowing me well enough at first and then not feeling right about things, and not that he said this but I took away from that to sort of mean that maybe in his mind if he didn't come then maybe it wasn't—he didn't need to feel guilty about that, that maybe with it not coming to completion that that was easier for him to rationalize."

—*Grand jury testimony,*
August 6, 1998

Revelation

"I have realized yesterday when Betty [Currie] told me you 'couldn't' see me, what's really going on—you want me out of your life. I guess the signs have been clear for awhile—not wanting to see me and rarely calling. I used to think it was simply you putting up walls."

—Letter to the President,
October 1997

Rituals

"It had sort of become actually a ritual sort of at this point, that we always kind of started out our meetings, that he was leaning against the closed door of the bathroom and I would rub his back, because he has a bad back. So, I used to always rub his back, and sometimes he'd rub my back. But I usually concentrated on his lower back because it was always bothering him. And, you know, then I'd usually move around and sort of just lovingly touch his chest and—"

—Deposition,
August 26, 1998

Romance

"Somebody accidentally knocked pizza on my jacket, so I went to go use the restroom to wash it off and as I was coming out of the restroom, the President was standing in Ms. Currie's doorway and said, 'You can come out this way.' So we went back into his back study area, actually, I think, in the bathroom or in the hallway right near the bathroom, and we were intimate."

—Grand jury testimony,
August 6, 1998

Running Mates

"I think I kind of said, 'Oh, I think we'd be a good team,' or something like that. And he, you know, he jokingly said, 'Well, what are we going to do when I'm 75 and I have to pee 25 times a day?' And I, you know, I told him that we'd deal with that. And it was—there was just this incredible connection."

—*Deposition,*
August 26, 1998

Safety

"I think that maybe there—there—maybe once or twice it had crossed my mind in some bizarre way because everybody's heard about the different—you know, sure there's the Marilyn Monroe theory. And so it—but it was not—it was not any factor of—that related to my actions."

—*Grand jury testimony,*
August 20, 1998

Seclusion

"It was really more the President choosing the hallway, I think, and it was—there weren't any windows there. It was the most secluded of all the places in the back office. Well, that's not true. The bathroom is the most secluded, I guess, because you can close the door."

—Grand jury testimony,
August 6, 1998

Secret Service

"From my understanding about what he [the President] testified to on Monday, not—just from the press accounts, is that this was a—that this was a service contract, that all I did was perform oral sex on him and that that's all that this relationship was. And it was a lot more than that to me and I thought it was a lot more than that."

—Grand jury testimony,
August 6, 1998

Security

"He was kissing me in the doorway between the back study, or the office, and the hallway, and I sort of opened my eyes and he was looking out of the window with his eyes wide open while he was kissing me and then I got mad because it wasn't very romantic. And so then he said, 'Well, I was just looking to see to make sure no one was out there.'"

—Grand jury testimony,
August 6, 1998

Security Measures

"Just a reminder to throw this away and *not* send it back to the staff secretary."

—Postscript to a letter to the President,
September 30, 1997

Self-Awareness

"All my life, everyone has always said that I am a difficult person for whom to shop."

—Letter to the President,
March 2, 1997

Self-Deception

"I want you in my life. I want to be able to enjoy my life, my work, lovers, friends and family. I want you to be a part of that."

—Letter to the President,
October 1997

Self-Determination

"I just knew he was in love with me, . . . and that's not, it's not something that . . . I would think easily. It's not a conclusion that I would come to easily at all. And it just—with the kind of person I am. . . . But just the way he looked at me and touched me, and the things he said, it just—it was so obvious to me. And it was shocking."

—Deposition,
August 26, 1998

Self-Esteem

"I am sorry that this has been such a bad experience. I will never forget what you said that night we fought on the phone—if you had known what I was really like you never would have gotten involved with me. I'm sure you're not the first person to have felt that way about me."

—Letter to the President,
October 1997

Self-Governance

"I have not said to myself, I have not said, 'You know what, Monica? This is a bad situation. You should not be involved with this person. It's just—there's no happiness here. You just need to get away from it.'"

—Telephone conversation with
Linda Tripp, between October 3 and
December 22, 1997

Self-Improvement

"Obviously there's—there's work that I need to do on myself. There are obviously issues that—that—you know, a single young woman doesn't have an affair with a married man because she's normal, quote-unquote. But I think most people have issues and that's just how mine manifested themselves. It's something I need to work on."

—Grand jury testimony,
August 20, 1998

Self-Pity

"What really hurts is that I cared so much about someone who just threw me away so quickly. I miss having someone to be with and enjoy me. Ohh, woe is me, woe is me, woe is me."

—*E-mail to a friend,*
November 19, 1997

Services Rendered

"There are a lot of people that could interpret that [performing oral sex while the President was on the telephone] as being sort of a, that being done in a servicing sort of manner, and it was more done in kind of an exciting sort of—I don't want to say erotic, but in a way that there was kind of this titillating like a secret, in a sense, in the same way sometimes that an affair, is, that, you know, when you are doing this and obviously there is kind of the irony that the person on the other line has no idea what's going on."

—*Deposition,*
August 26, 1998

Sex

"Having sex is having intercourse."

*—Telephone conversation with
Linda Tripp, between October 3 and
December 22, 1997*

Signal

"I mean, the President doesn't wear the same tie twice in one week, so—I didn't know what it meant, but it was some sort of a reminder to me."

*—Grand jury testimony,
August 6, 1998*

Significance

"I also cannot ignore what we have shared together. I don't care what you say, *(redacted)* never would have seen that raw, intense sexuality that I saw a few times— watching your mouth on my breast or looking in your eyes while you explored the depth of my sex. Instead it would have been a routine encounter void of anything but a sexual release."

—Undated draft of a letter to the President recovered from a deleted computer file, 1997

Sincerity

"He was talking about that . . . he cherishes the time that he had with me, which seemed a little bit odd to me at that time. . . . I didn't feel like he really knew me. We had spent time talking, . . . and you know, he had asked some questions and I offered a lot of information about myself. But he didn't seem to ask probing questions, when you're trying to get to know someone. So, it seemed a little bit odd to me that he would sort of cherish this time, when he, you know, when I felt like he didn't really even know me yet."

—Deposition,
August 26, 1998

Slavery

"I cannot be free when I [*sic*] constantly stressing about why you haven't called me, returned my calls, wanted to see me, etc."

—*Letter to the President,*
October 1997

Social Security

"As I'm sure everyone can imagine, that this is a kind of relationship that you keep quiet, and we both wanted to be careful being in the White House. Whenever I would visit him during . . . my tenure at the White House, we always—unless it was sort of a chance meeting on a weekend and then we ended up back in the office—we would usually plan that I would either bring papers, or one time we had actually accidentally bumped into each other in the hall and went from that way, so then we planned to do that again because that seemed to work well. But we always— there was always some sort of a cover."

—*Grand jury testimony,*
August 6, 1998

Solidarity

"I thought he's just the kind of person that's going to wear this tie to tug on my emotional strings one last time before I go into the grand jury and say this under oath. And he didn't. And him wearing it the day I came to testify sort of having to know that I wasn't going to see it until the end of the day, to me was just kind of—you know, hey, you had to do what you had to do."

—Grand jury testimony,
August 20, 1998

Souvenirs

"I didn't keep this dress as a souvenir. I was going to wear it on Thanksgiving and my cousins, who I always try to look skinny for because they are all skinny—and I know it sounds stupid. And when I told Linda [Tripp] I was thinking about wearing the dress, she discouraged me. She brought me one of her jackets from her thinner closet. And so it wasn't a souvenir. I was going to wear it again."

—Grand jury testimony,
August 6, 1998

Stability

"Any normal person would have walked away from this and said, 'He doesn't call me, he doesn't want to see me—screw it. It doesn't matter.' I can't let go of you."

—Letter to the President,
October 1997

Stain Removal

"And at that point I noticed it and I kind of thought, oh, this is dirty, it needs to get cleaned. And then I remembered that I had worn it the last time I saw the President, and I believe it was at that point that I thought to myself, oh, no."

—Grand jury testimony,
August 6, 1998

Stamina

"I'm tired of having to pussyfoot around everybody."

—Telephone conversation with
Linda Tripp, between October 3 and
December 22, 1997

State of the Union

"I am tired of crying and analyzing why you don't call me, why everything is the way it is."

—*Letter to the President,*
October 1997

Statistics

"Okay, this happens in everyday life. People stop liking each other you know. Women every day—I'm sure every minute of every day somebody is getting dumped."

—*Telephone conversation with*
Linda Tripp, between October 3 and
December 22, 1997

Stature

"Before I performed oral sex on him, I wanted him to touch my genitals with his genitals. And so we sort of had tried to do that, but because he's really tall and he couldn't bend because of his knee, it didn't really work."

—Deposition,
August 28, 1998

Status

"What if your grandma right now told you she had an affair with the President? How vastly would that change your grandma's life?"

—Telephone conversation with
Linda Tripp, between October 3 and
December 22, 1997

Strategy

"He had told me earlier on that he was usually around on the weekends and that it was okay to come see him on the weekends. So he would call and we would arrange either to bump into each other in the hall or that I would bring papers to the office."

—Grand jury testimony,
August 6, 1998

Success

"I had a view of—and this is sort of my view with work is that you get a lot more done and people are a lot more willing to help you when you have a personal interaction with them."

—Grand jury testimony,
August 20, 1998

Sunglasses

"I had teased him [the President] for a long time about the different sunglasses that he was wearing in public. And so then I bought him a normal pair of sunglasses, and so we had just sort of had—this was a long running joke with us, so he bought me these really funny looking sunglasses and we both were putting them on and joking around goofing off."

—Grand jury testimony,
August 6, 1998

Support

"I was waiting for the President in the back study and then he hobbled in because he was on crutches. And we were, we were in the back office. . . . I think he had put his crutches down and he was kind of leaning on me. So, I was holding him, you know, I mean, sort of romantically but at the same time literally holding him."

—Deposition,
August 26, 1998

Survival

"So it's over. I don't know what I will do now but I can't wait any more and I can't go through all of this crap anymore. In some ways I hope I never hear from him again because he'll just lead me on because he doesn't have the balls to tell me the truth. I kind of phase in and out of being sad—as to be expected but I'll survive. What other choice do I have?"

—E-mail to a friend,
September 16, 1997

Suspicion

"I was under the impression that—that Mr. Jordan kind of knew with a wink and a nod that I was having a relationship with the President, that it was never—he and I never discussed it, but I thought it might be possible."

—Grand jury testimony,
August 6, 1998

Sweet Nothings

"I mean, I think that there were always things being said, but not necessarily in a conversational form."

—Deposition,
August 26, 1998

Symbolism

"I hope you know how very grateful I am for these gifts, especially your gift of friendship. I will treasure them all . . . always."

—Letter to the President,
March 2, 1997

Sympathy

"I get sad when I need some TLC and I can't get it. I haven't made the circle of friends here in DC like I had in Portland where if I just needed a guy I had 3 or 4 male friends on whom I could call. Here it seems that most of the guys in my life I have dated so of course, there's always baggage involved. I think I'm not happy here in DC and I'm not really sure what to do about it. So in a nutshell . . . I'm sad."

—E-mail to a friend,
September 16, 1997

Tact

"My dad didn't know anything about the relationship and when he went on his—the few interviews he did, he was telling the truth when he said he didn't know. But out of respect for the President and the presidency, he didn't say—he could have easily said if this is true; X, Y, and Z about the President, and I think that because my family didn't start a huge uproar about how wrong or improper or inappropriate it was for a 50-year-old man to be having a relationship with a young woman, we afforded him that, that was one less headache that he had to deal with, and I think he could have acknowledged that."

—Grand jury testimony,
August 20, 1998

Technology

"God this e-mail system sucks so much!!!!"

—E-mail to a friend,
September 16, 1997

Tension

"A person can only handle so might [*sic*] anxiety and stress."

—Unsent letter to the President,
September 1997

Terms of Endearment

"I had thought that he had forgotten my name before, because I had seen him in the hall a few times and he kept calling me 'Kiddo.' So, so, I sort of reiterated my—I said my name again to him. You know, I said, you know, 'It's Monica Lewinsky, President Kiddo,' you know. And he said, 'I know your name.' And he told me that he had tried to call me and that—he said, 'but you're not in the book; I even spelled your last name right.' So, it was, it was really funny. It was cute."

—*Deposition,*
August 26, 1998

Terror

"I burst into tears. I was—it was very scary. I mean, it just—sort of my worst nightmare, or I had thought until that point, was being subpoenaed in this case. So I was pretty upset."

—*Grand jury testimony,*
August 6, 1998

Theater

"When I saw *Rent* I was saddened during the number Mimi sang, 'Goodbye Love.' Not for the reasons the composer wanted me to be, but because I was thinking about you and how I didn't want us to get to a point where I would have to say 'goodbye handsome.'"

—*Letter to the President,*
October 1997

Ties

"Almost all of our conversations included something about my ties.... I used to bug him about wearing one of my ties because then I knew I was close to his heart."

—Grand jury testimony,
August 6, 1998

Time

"It's really hard for me to estimate the time."

—Deposition,
August 26, 1998

Titanic

"I think it was Saturday night when I got home from the movies and I had seen the Titanic that weekend and it just was—just brought up a lot of feelings and thoughts for me that I put on—that I put on paper. . . . Because I was angry about seeing the picture with them romantic."

—Grand jury testimony,
August 6, 1998

Totality

"I go to work every day *(crying)* and I just *(crying)*, I'm trying to keep it together and I just can't."

—Telephone conversation with
Linda Tripp, between October 3 and
December 22, 1997

Transcendence

"I always felt that we sort of just, we both really went to a, to a whole other place together sexually."

—*Deposition,*
August 26, 1998

Trickle-Down Economics

"I told him that I really cared about him and he told me that he didn't want to get addicted to me and he didn't want me to get addicted to him, and we embraced at that point and that's—I mean, it was—it's just a little spot down here and little tiny spot up here and—"

—*Grand jury testimony,*
August 6, 1998

True Nature

"Toward the end of the letter I softened up again and was back to my mushy self."

—Grand jury testimony,
August 6, 1998

Trust

"He stopped me before he came, and I told him that I wanted to, to complete that. And he said that, that he needed to wait until he trusted me more."

—Deposition,
August 26, 1998

Truth

"I thought he had a beautiful soul. I just thought he was just this incredible person and when I looked at him I saw a little boy and—I don't know what the truth is anymore."

—Grand jury testimony,
August 20, 1998

Trysts

"I'd say they mainly took place in that hallway, but there were occasions on which we were intimate in the office and then also in the bathroom."

—Grand jury testimony,
August 6, 1998

Understanding

"When Betty [Currie] called, then she said, you know, 'I understand you have something to give me.' It was very vague. And I understood—I mean, to me, that meant from this conversation that we had had that I should sort of—you know, give some of the gifts."

—Grand jury testimony,
August 20, 1998

Unemployment

"My initial reaction was that I was never going to see the President again. I mean, my relationship with him would be over."

—Grand jury testimony,
August 6, 1998,
on her reaction to losing
her job at the White House

Upheaval

"Let's just say the Paula Jones thing had gone ahead and I had somehow been dragged into that, just being associated with it and it being difficult and maybe he— maybe it was going to seriously alter a kind of friendship or relationship that we had, you know?"

—*Grand jury testimony,*
August 6, 1998

Uprisings

"And actually at one point during this encounter, I think someone came into the, to the Oval Office and he, you know, zipped up real quickly and went out and came back in, and . . . I just remember laughing because he had walked out there and he was visibly aroused, and I just thought it was funny. I mean, it wouldn't, it wouldn't necessarily be visible to anyone who just walked in because they wouldn't be looking at that, but it was just funny to me."

—Deposition,
August 26, 1998

Urban Renewal

"I truly know how difficult it can be to assimilate to a new city."

—Letter to a friend,
May 18, 1997

Validity

"And so how could I know the truth of my love for someone if it was based on him being an actor?"

—Grand jury testimony,
August 20, 1998

Vernon Jordan

"I attributed things to Mr. Jordan that weren't true because I knew that it had leverage with Linda [Tripp] and that a lot of those things that I said got him into a lot of trouble."

—Grand jury testimony,
August 6, 1998

Visibility

"You know, I also wanted to try to see the President. So, I mean, I did make efforts to try to see him in the hall or something like that."

—Grand jury testimony,
August 20, 1998

Vision

"He always used to push the hair out of my face."

—*Grand jury testimony,*
August 6, 1998

Vocabulary

"He would always sort of—what's the word I'm looking for? Kind of validate what I was feeling by telling me something that I don't necessarily know is true."

—*Grand jury testimony,*
August 6, 1998

Vulnerability

"I think that—the President seemed to pay attention to me and I paid attention to him and I think people were wary of his weaknesses, maybe, and thought—in my opinion, I mean, this is—I think that people— they didn't want to look at him and think that he could be responsible for anything, so it had to all be my fault, that I was—I was stalking him or I was making advances toward him. You know, as they've said, I wore inappropriate clothes, which is absolutely not true. I'm not really sure."

—*Grand jury testimony,*
August 20, 1998

Walt Whitman

"I have only read excerpts from 'Leaves of Grass' before—never in its entirety or in such a beautifully bound edition. Like Shakespeare, Whitman's writings are so timeless. I find solace in works from the past that remain profound and somehow always poignant. Whitman is so rich that one must read him like one tastes a fine wine or good cigar—take it in, roll it in your mouth, and savor it!"

—Letter to the President,
March 2, 1997

Weaknesses

"No one likes to have their weaknesses splayed out for the entire world, you know, but . . . I'd rather you understand where I'm coming from, you know, and you'd probably have to know me better and know my whole journey to how I got here from birth to now to really understand it."

—Grand jury testimony,
August 20, 1998

Weirdos

"He [Presidential Advisor Harold Ickes]—well, he—he's just strange. And he—I'm sorry. He would—you know, you could be the only person in the hall and you would pass Mr. Ickes in the hall and he would just glare at you. You know. And I'd say, 'Hello,' you know, as you would imagine you're supposed to do and he'd just glare at you and walk past you. And I thought that was strange. Call me weird."

—Grand jury testimony,
August 6, 1998

White House

"Who can put a price on working there? I mean, I was thinking when I was in New York, I will never work in a place as beautiful . . . I will never work in as a prestigious place."

—Telephone conversation with Linda Tripp,
between October 3 and December 22, 1997

Wisdom

"He didn't want to. The President said that he—that at his age, that there was too much of a consequence in doing that [having sexual intercourse] and that when I got to be his age I would understand. But I wasn't happy with that."

—Grand jury testimony,
August 6, 1998

World Peace

"I know that what is going on in the world takes precedence, but I don't think what I have asked you for is unreasonable. I can't help but to have hurt feelings when I sent you a note last week and this week, and you still haven't seen me or called me."

—Letter to the President,
November 12, 1997

Yin-Yang

"I can't understand how you could be so kind and so cruel to me. When I think of all the times you filled my heart and my soul with sunshine and then think of the times you made me cry for hours and want to die, I feel nauseous."

—Letter to the President,
December 1997

Youth

"My mom is younger than he is."

—Telephone conversation with
Linda Tripp, between October 3 and
December 22, 1997

Visit author Joey Green
on the Internet at:

www.wackyuses.com